Caring for Your
Hamster

Jill Foran

Weigl Publishers Inc.

Project Coordinator
Diana Marshall

Design and Layout
Warren Clark
Katherine Phillips

Copy Editor
Jennifer Nault

Photo Research
Gayle Murdoff

Published by Weigl Publishers Inc.
123 South Broad Street, Box 227
Mankato, MN 56002 USA
Web site: www.weigl.com

Library of Congress Cataloging-in-Publication Data available upon request from the
publisher. Fax (507) 388-2746 for the attention of the Publishing Records Department.

ISBN 1-59036-066-4

Printed in Canada
1 2 3 4 5 6 7 8 9 0   06 05 04 03 02

Locate the hamster paw prints throughout the book to find useful tips on caring for your pet.

Photograph and Text Credits
Every reasonable effort has been made to trace ownership and to obtain permission
to reprint copyright material. The publishers would be pleased to have any errors
or omissions brought to their attention so that they may be corrected in
subsequent printings.

Cover: hamster eating (Eric Ilasenko Photo/Digital); **Behling and Johnson
Photography:** page 25; **Comstock Images:** page 23 top; **Corel Corporation:** page
8; **Hammertime Publications:** page 27; **Lorraine Hill:** title page, pages 3, 5 bottom,
6 left, 7 left, 7 middle, 7 right, 10 top, 10 bottom, 11 top, 17 top, 17 bottom, 18/19, 22,
23 top, 23 bottom, 31; **Eric Ilasenko Photo/Digital:** pages 6 right, 9, 11 bottom, 13,
15, 16, 20, 21 bottom, 28, 30; **Preston Lyon/MaXx Images Inc.:** pages 24, 26; **Reneé
Stockdale:** pages 4, 5 top, 12, 14, 21 top.

Wiebe, Trina. *Hamsters Don't Glow in the Dark*. Montreal: Lobster Press, 2000.

Contents

Hamsters and Happiness

Hamsters make great pets. Their soft fur, adorable faces, and small size have made hamsters popular household companions in many parts of the world. Not only are hamsters cute and cuddly, they are also easy to care for. They are clean, cheap, and take up very little room. In addition, hamsters are very energetic. They provide their owners with countless hours of enjoyment.

Try to play with your hamster in the evening, when he is awake and alert.

Hamsters need a clean cage to live in, plenty of food and water, and regular exercise.

Even though a hamster is a fun pet, looking after one is a large responsibility. Once you have a pet hamster, you must care for him for the rest of his life. This means that you must give him the things that will keep him happy and healthy. Hamsters require food, shelter, grooming, and plenty of playtime. Hamsters also need some privacy during the day.

■ Hamsters are nocturnal animals. This means that they sleep during the day and are active at night.

Fascinating Facts

- The word "hamster" comes from the German word *hamstern*, which means "to **hoard**." Hamsters hoard food in case it is not available later.
- Of all the small pets in the world, hamsters are the most popular. More people own hamsters than chinchillas, ferrets, gerbils, guinea pigs, mice, rabbits, or rats.

Pet Profiles

More than twenty types of hamsters live in the wild. From the large common hamster to the mouse-like Chinese hamster, these wild animals live mostly in the plains and deserts of Central Asia. Of all the different types of hamsters, only five are commonly kept as pets.

If you put two Syrian hamsters in the same cage, they will likely fight viciously.

CHINESE

- Mouse-like appearance
- Slender body
- Long tail
- Grayish-brown coat
- Black-tipped ears
- Dark stripe down their back
- Hard to breed because the females are very aggressive

SYRIAN

- Most common type of pet hamster
- Wide range of colors
- Many different **coat** lengths, from long-haired to hairless
- Only the males are long-haired
- Hairless feet
- **Solitary**
- Fierce fighter
- Also called golden hamsters because some have gold-colored fur

The most common **domesticated** hamster is the Syrian hamster. Over the years, people have discovered that Syrian hamsters can be **bred** to have different color and fur variations. The appearance of these large hamsters can vary a great deal. This makes Syrian hamsters very popular among pet owners.

DJUNGARIAN

- Also known as Campbell's Russian
- A dwarf hamster
- Plump, round body
- Fuzzy fur
- Fine black line running from ears to tail
- Very friendly
- Furry feet
- Like to live in pairs provided they are introduced at a young age

ROBOROVSKI'S

- Smallest type of pet dwarf hamster
- Lively and fast
- Calm temperament
- Golden-orange in color with white belly
- Fur over eyes is white, giving them distinctive white "eyebrows"

SIBERIAN

- Also known as Winter White Russian
- A dwarf hamster
- Originally from southwest Siberia, where they lived on the grassy slopes
- Gray and white, with dark markings on nose, ears, and tail
- Fur turns white in winter
- Black stripe down back
- Sociable; mixes well with own type and other types of hamsters

Hamster History

Hamsters are members of a large group of animals called **rodents**. Some types of hamsters have been around for centuries. The first recorded discovery of the Syrian hamster happened in the late 1700s near a place called Aleppo, in the deserts of Syria. Syrian hamsters were found in **burrows**, many feet under the sand's surface. Years later, in 1839, a **zoologist** named George Robert Waterhouse presented a female golden hamster to the London Zoological Society. This hamster was also captured near Aleppo. For years after Waterhouse's presentation, no one could find further evidence of the wild Syrian hamsters. People believed they had become **extinct**.

Hamsters are related to other rodents, such as the prairie dog.

Fascinating Facts

- The rodent group, which includes mice, squirrels, beavers, and prairie dogs, is the most varied of all the animal groups.
- In Syria, where wild hamsters are common, farmers dig into hamster's burrows. There, they find up to 60 pounds of grain stored by the hamsters for the winter.
- Hamsters were brought to the United States in 1938.

Beware of pairs. Putting a male and a female hamster in one cage will result in many baby hamsters.

In 1930, a doctor named Israel Aharoni captured a mother Syrian hamster and her eleven babies. These hamsters had also been living near Aleppo, burrowed deep under the Syrian desert. Although most of the hamsters that Doctor Aharoni captured either died or escaped, he managed to keep three. Within a short while, these three hamsters had produced hundreds of baby hamsters.

■Today, almost all domesticated Syrian hamsters are descended from Doctor Aharoni's three original hamsters.

Life Cycle

Hamsters have a life span of 2 to 4 years. Although this is not a long time, most hamsters remain healthy and strong throughout their lives. No matter what stage of life your hamster is at, she will depend on you to give her proper care and love.

Newborn Hamsters

Newborn hamsters are called puppies. A hamster is tiny and almost completely helpless when he is born. He has no fur, and cannot see or hear. While a newborn hamster cannot move well, he is able to pull himself along by his front feet. If your pet hamster has just given birth, be sure to watch her carefully. Young or shy mother hamsters may eat their young if they sense danger or are disturbed.

Mature Hamsters

By 5 to 6 months of age, a hamster is full-grown. He is now independent, active, and curious. Adult hamsters need plenty of toys in their cages to keep them busy. Extra vitamins are sometimes necessary for senior hamsters.

Fascinating Facts

- Hamsters have the shortest pregnancy of all animals. The period from mating to birth is only 16 days.

Two to Three Weeks Old

By 2 to 3 weeks, a hamster has a soft, furry coat. He is alert and moving around. He is also starting to eat solid food instead of just his mother's milk, and is learning to hoard food.

Five Weeks Old

By 5 weeks of age, a hamster is ready to live on his own, away from his mother and littermates. If you do not give your hamster a home of his own, he may fight with the other hamsters. A female hamster is now old enough to have puppies of her own.

Picking Your Pet

Before choosing a hamster, there are many factors to consider. Learning all you can about hamsters will help you choose the one that is right for you. The following questions should be answered before you make your pet selection.

Which Type of Hamster Should I Get?

Syrian hamsters are the most widely available type of hamster. Syrian hamsters are quite large, which makes them easy to handle. They like to live alone. Dwarf hamsters and Chinese hamsters are better choices if you want to keep more than one hamster in a cage. However, these types are harder to handle than Syrian hamsters because they are much smaller and can move very fast.

When looking for a hamster, be sure to visit the pet store or breeder in the evening. This is when the hamsters will be awake.

■ Be sure to keep other family pets away from your new pet hamster.

How Old Should the Hamster Be?

There are many adult hamsters that need good homes. Hamsters do not live for very long, so it may a good idea to get one that is young. If you choose a baby hamster, make sure that he is at least 4 weeks old.

How Should I Pick and Prepare for My New Hamster?

Before picking out a new hamster, consider the safety of your home. Hamsters cannot defend themselves against large animals, such as cats and dogs. When you are ready to buy your hamster, be sure to go to a trustworthy pet store or breeder. Examine the hamster you have chosen to be sure he is healthy. His ears, nose, mouth, and bottom should be clean, and his eyes should be clear. Also, check that the hamster's coat is shiny, and that his skin is healthy.

■ When buying your pet hamster, look carefully at all the hamsters. Try to pick the one that seems the liveliest.

Fascinating Facts

- Djungarian hamsters were not widely sold as pets until 1995.
- Hamsters are solitary animals. This means that they usually live alone.

Gearing Up

Before bringing a hamster home, you will need to be prepared with some special equipment. You should have a large, secure cage for your new hamster. The best type to buy is a wire cage with a plastic bottom. These cages provide good **ventilation**, and the wires provide excellent climbing bars for your hamster. You will also need to line the floor of the cage with wood shavings. Sawdust and cedar wood shavings should be avoided as they may cause health problems in some hamsters. The wood shavings in your pet hamster's cage should be spread at least 2 inches thick so that your pet has something to burrow in.

Cotton wool should never be used for your hamster's bedding. If eaten, it can block her stomach and make her ill.

■ Your hamster's cage should include a little house for sleeping in, a heavy food dish, a water bottle, and plenty of nesting materials.

Pet supply stores sell all kinds of hamster toys, including plastic tunnels, climbing trees, and gnawing logs. You can also use materials from your home as toys. An empty toilet paper roll makes a great tunnel. Finally, every hamster should have an exercise wheel. Be sure that the bars of the exercise wheel are not too far apart. This will prevent your hamster's tiny paws from getting stuck.

■ Hamsters are active animals. To keep your hamster fit, be sure to provide her with toys.

Fascinating Facts

- In the wild, hamsters will often dig tunnels as long as 11 yards.
- Hamsters have been known to chew their way through wooden cages.

Feeding Your Hamster

Hamsters are omnivores. This means that they eat both plants and animals. In the wild, hamsters munch on grains, roots, insects, and whatever else they can find. Although your pet hamster does not need to eat insects, she will require a varied, balanced diet.

Every morning, remove any leftover fresh food from your hamster's cage. Otherwise, the food may spoil.

Hamsters enjoy a variety of fresh fruits and vegetables, such as grapes, and pieces of apple, carrot, and celery.

■ Commercial hamster foods provide a good mix of dry foods for your hamster, including grains, vegetables, and seeds.

The best time to feed your hamster is in the early evening, when she is at her most active. You only need to feed her once a day. Do not worry if it looks like your hamster still seems hungry after she has eaten the food in her dish. She has likely hidden food in other parts of her cage. She will hoard the food and eat it later.

Fascinating Facts

- Chocolate, raw beans, citrus fruits, iceberg lettuce, and tomatoes can all be poisonous to hamsters.
- Hamsters need a fresh supply of water at all times. Without water, hamsters can become very ill. Water bottles with dispensers are useful because they do not tip and they keep the water clean.

Built for Burrows

All hamsters have certain features in common. Whether your pet is a large Syrian hamster or a tiny Roborovski's hamster, his physical characteristics are much like those of all other hamsters in the world. From their eyes right down to their paws, hamsters' features are suited to life underground.

All hamsters have scent **glands** on their hips. These glands produce a musky liquid that allows hamsters to mark their territory and to identify themselves to other hamsters.

A hamster's front paws have four clawed toes. The front paws are used for grooming and digging, as well as for holding food and emptying the cheek pouches. The hind feet, which provide a strong grip, each have five toes.

= SYRIAN

Hamsters have thin, delicate ears and very good hearing. They can hear all kinds of sounds, including sounds that humans cannot hear.

Although they have large, bulging eyes, hamsters have a poor sense of sight. They cannot see objects at close range, and they are nearly blind in bright daylight. Hamsters see best in dim light.

Whiskers help a hamster feel her way around. They act as sensors by allowing a hamster to detect objects in her environment.

Hamsters have an excellent sense of smell. Hamsters use their noses as guides to identify many things, including food and other hamsters. If they are handled often, hamsters will be able to recognize their owners by their scent.

Hamsters have pouches inside both cheeks. These pouches stretch from the cheeks to the shoulder and hold large amounts of food. The skin lining the pouches is dry and rough. This keeps the food from falling out of the mouth or from being swallowed.

A hamster has a large mouth, with sixteen teeth. All hamsters have long upper and lower **incisors** at the front of their mouths. They also have eight molars that help them chew food.

Hamster Housecleaning

Hamsters are very clean animals. They keep their homes tidy and organized. In order to help your hamster keep his home in good shape, you should clean out his cage at least once a week. A hamster living in a clean, tidy cage is more likely to live a long and happy life.

Your hamster's food dish and water bottle should be cleaned every day.

■ Hamsters usually choose different areas in their cage for sleeping, storing food, and going to the bathroom.

To clean your hamster's cage, empty out the contents, but save some of the wood shavings, bedding, and hoarded food. Scrub the entire cage with hot, soapy water. You may also spray the inside of the cage with a special **disinfectant**. As hamsters are sensitive to scents, you should ask a **veterinarian** for a safe, mild disinfectant for your hamster's cage. Remember to put the old bedding, food, and shavings back inside the cage. This will help your hamster feel more at ease in his freshly cleaned home.

■■■When the cage is clean and dry, spread fresh wood shavings along its floor.

Fascinating Facts

- A hamster's front teeth never stop growing. They must be filed down by gnawing.
- Bathing a hamster is dangerous because it removes the hamster's natural oils.

Healthy and Happy

Hamsters are generally healthy pets. If they are properly cared for, they will rarely get sick. To keep your hamster healthy, be sure to feed him a balanced diet and clean his cage regularly. An exercise wheel is the best way to ensure that your pet hamster stays active and energetic. Some hamsters become ill when they are put into stressful situations, such as too much handling or loud noises. To prevent this, leave your hamster alone during the day and keep his cage in a quiet area of the house.

Examine your pet hamster regularly for signs of illness. Signs of a sick hamster include loss of appetite, inactivity, a dull coat, sneezing, a wet tail, and a runny nose or eyes. If you notice any of these symptoms, you should contact your veterinarian.

Hamsters may become sick if they are fed too much fresh food.

A hamster can run up to 8 miles a day on her exercise wheel.

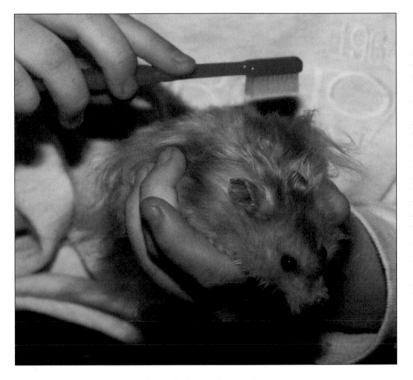

Hamsters do a good job keeping themselves clean. They wash and groom themselves regularly. This means that you do not have to groom or bathe your hamster. However, if you have a long-haired hamster, you should gently brush his coat regularly with a very soft toothbrush. This will keep his fur from becoming **matted**.

 It is important to brush long-haired hamsters. Hamsters should be brushed at night, when they are awake and alert.

Fascinating Facts

- Hamsters can catch colds and the flu from people.
- Hamsters are sensitive to temperature. If they become too cold, they will **hibernate**.
- Hamsters spend much of their waking time grooming themselves. They use their tongues, their teeth, and their paws to keep their fur in good condition. They bend into all sorts of positions to reach every part of their body.

Handling Your Hamster

Getting your new hamster used to you will take time and patience. Although you may want to start playing with your pet right away, this is not a good idea. Handling your hamster too soon may scare her or even cause her to bite you. Allow your pet a few days to get used to her new home. Start by trying to feed her out of your hand. Once your hamster is eating from your fingers, let her sniff your hand so that she knows your scent. When she seems comfortable with you, you can try to pick her up.

Make sure that you are holding your hamster close to the ground so that if he falls, he will not get hurt.

■ It is important to slowly and carefully introduce yourself to your new pet hamster.

Pet Peeves

Hamsters do not like:
- being startled when sleeping
- being handled or played with during the daytime
- eating sharp or sticky foods that get stuck in their cheek pouches
- being squeezed or held too tightly, especially when their cheek pouches are full of food

To pick up your hamster, place one hand gently over her back, and wrap your fingers around her body. Cup your other hand under your hamster to scoop her up. When your hamster is used to being picked up, she will begin to walk across your hands. Gradually, she will become comfortable with being held.

When your hamster is out of her cage and in a safe area of the house, you can begin to teach her tricks. Play between pet hamsters and their owners is very important. Try dangling a treat of food over your hamster's head. Soon, she will stand on her haunches to reach the treat.

■ Holding your hamster in this way will make him feel warm, safe, and secure.

Fascinating Facts

- A hamster's cheek pouches can hold up to 0.63 ounces of food.
- Hamsters do not have belly buttons.

Hamsters and Humans

Humans have been keeping hamsters as pets since the 1940s. For more than 60 years, these small animals have brought joy and amusement to many homes. People who own hamsters are often very proud of their furry companions. Some owners enjoy entering their hamsters into professional hamster shows. In such competitions, hamsters are judged and given prizes for their features, such as the quality of their coat. Hamster shows take place in many parts of the world.

■ Hamster owners love to show their pets to friends and family members.

Fascinating Facts

- Many hamsters blink one eye at a time.
- Hamster associations offer information about hamster breed standards. These standards help pet owners judge whether their pet hamsters can be shown at a competition.

Over the years, many hamsters have appeared in films and television shows. They have guest starred in shows ranging from *The Brady Bunch* to *The Simpsons*. Perhaps the best-loved hamster to appear on television is Hammy the Hamster. Hammy the Hamster lives in an old boot on a beautiful riverbank. He and his friends have many adventures. Each show teaches the audience to appreciate the natural environment and to be respectful of all animals.

In stories, in films, and in television shows, hamsters capture people's hearts through their mischief and energy.

■ Hammy the Hamster appears in a popular television program called *Once Upon A Hamster.*

The Great Escape

In *Hamsters Don't Glow in the Dark*, Abby is excited when she finds out she has been chosen to bring the class hamster home for a week. In this story, as in many other hamster tales, adventure begins with the hamster. Mr. Nibbles, the hamster, becomes better friends with Abby's dog. To make matters worse, it is soon discovered that Mr. Nibbles has escaped. Abby goes on one adventure after the other in search of her frisky friend, the pet hamster.

From Trina Wiebe's *Hamsters Don't Glow in the Dark*.

Pet Puzzlers

What do you know about hamsters?
If you can answer the following
questions correctly, you may
be ready to own a pet hamster.

Q Should you give
your pet hamster
a bath?

Hamsters should never be
bathed. Bathing removes
a hamster's natural oils.
Leave your hamster to
clean and groom himself.
He will do this using his
tongue and paws.

Q How many years
do pet hamsters
usually live?

Hamsters only live between 2
and 4 years. Despite this short
life span, hamsters usually
stay strong and healthy
throughout their lives.

Q When is the best time of day to feed a hamster?

The best time to feed a hamster is in the early evening. This is the time of day when hamsters are most active and alert.

Q Why is it recommended to leave your hamster alone in the morning?

Hamsters are nocturnal animals. This means that they sleep during most of the day, and play and eat at night.

Q Why do hamsters have cheek pouches?

Hamsters store large amounts of food in their cheek pouches. Some of this food is spat out and hoarded, to be eaten later.

Q Where and when was the first known hamster found?

The first known hamster was found in the deserts of Syria, in the late 1700s.

Holler for Your Hamster

Before you buy your pet hamster, write down some hamster names that you like. Some names may work better for a female hamster. Others may suit a male hamster. Here are just a few suggestions:

Buster

Sandy

Minney

Fluffy

Snowflake

Teddy

Patches

Ginger

Hammy

Cheeky

Frequently Asked Questions

How can I keep my hamster from escaping from his cage?

Hamsters are adventurous. They will always try to find ways to get out of their cages. At some point, most hamsters will succeed in escaping. You can try to prevent this by making sure that the door of your pet's cage closes securely, and that the cage has no other wide openings. If your hamster does escape, the best time to look for him is at night, when he is likely to be active. Try catching him by placing food and bedding out for him.

Should I breed my hamster?

Unless you know that you can find homes for many puppies, it is not a good idea to breed your hamster. A female hamster normally gives birth to between five and seven puppies. For the first few weeks of their lives, puppies can stay with their mother and siblings in one cage. Within about 2 months, each puppy will need a cage of his or her own.

Is it safe to let my hamster run around my room?

Many hamster owners let their hamsters out of their cages once in a while. This is fine, as long as you keep a close eye on your pet. You must make sure that the room your hamster is exploring is closed off from the rest of the house. If you have other pets, make sure none of them are in the room with your hamster. To be safe, it may be best to let your hamster run inside a plastic exercise ball.

More Information

Animal Organizations

You can help hamsters stay healthy and happy by learning more about them. Many organizations are dedicated to teaching people how to care for and protect their pet pals. For more hamster information, write to the following organizations:

American Hamster Association
P.O. Box 457
Leavenworth, KS 66048

Humane Society of the United States
2100 L Street N.W.
Washington, DC 20037

Web Sites

To answer more of your hamster questions, go online and surf to the following Web sites:

Care for Animals
www.avma.org/careforanimals/
animatedjourneys/animatedfl.asp

HamsterLand
www.hamsterland.com

Pet Web Site
www.petwebsite.com/
about_hamsters.htm

Words to Know

bred: mated; sexually reproduced
burrows: holes or tunnels deep in the ground
coat: an animal's fur
disinfectant: a chemical used to kill harmful germs
domesticated: used to living among people; no longer wild
extinct: no longer in existence
glands: special organs that produce scents
hibernate: sleep through the winter

hoard: save for future use
incisors: teeth used for cutting or gnawing
matted: tangled, knotted; having clumps of fur
rodents: mammals with teeth designed for nibbling or gnawing
solitary: living without companions
ventilation: constant fresh air
veterinarian: animal doctor
zoologist: a scientist who studies animals

Index